Home Generator: Selecting, Sizing And Connecting

The Complete Guide

Lazar Rozenblat

TO MY BELOVED PARENTS
OF BLESSED MEMORY

Third Edition

Contents

INTRODUCTION

In spite of all the technological progress, the frequency of power outages in U.S. and the number of people affected keeps increasing. Since most power distribution lines in the U.S. still use overhead wires, and because of the deteriorating infrastructure of our electric grid, this trend will likely continue. While brief rolling blackouts may be just an annoyance, power loss for days or even weeks can be costly and even life-threatening. Besides spoiled food, loss of heat in the winter or air conditioning in the summer, an ordinary outage may result in a flooded basement, frozen pipes, inoperative security system, and lost business. A private backup power system can let you continue using selected appliances and lights when the grid fails, or supply electricity to the entire house. Unfortunately, for many homeowners who do not have a background in electrical engineering, choosing, sizing and connecting a backup system can be challenging. What type is best for prolonged power outages? How to accurately determine the required wattage? Is my existing natural gas service sufficient to run a standby generator? How do I safely connect a portable generator to the house wiring? These are some of the commonly asked questions.

This guide written by a power electronics engineer will answer these and many other questions and provide you with the practical information that you need to know in order to choose the right emergency power system for your needs. The guide covers standby and portable electric generators in minute detail. It also presents an overview of battery-based systems. For each type of electric generators the book provides principles of operation, pros and cons, lesser known details, charts with comparative characteristics of the popular brands, cost estimation, sizing and wiring options. In conclusion the author offers his generator picks depending on your requirements and budget.

OVERVIEW OF DIFFERENT BACKUP POWER SYSTEMS

Emergency power for the home can be generated in a number of ways depending on the energy source and on the device that converts it to electricity. The chart in the next page outlines your main options. The numbers and features in this chart are for basic reference only-- they are provided just to give you an idea of what you can expect from a typical system available on the market. The actual installation cost of course will depend on many factors, such as wattage, project complexity and the length of the lines to run. Note that grid-tie solar and wind systems usually come with various rebates and incentives not reflected in this chart. For all battery-based systems the runtime and cost will depend on the size of the battery bank.

In my view, **electric generators** (portable and standby) are the most practical solutions for homeowners. All battery-based systems with a realistic size of a battery bank can provide only short runtime (see page 47). They may be useful if you want to protect yourself against brief rolling blackouts or if your power consumption is very low, but they are not suitable for extended outages. Note that conventional solar-powered systems for on-grid applications are batteryless. Contrary to a popular misconception, they are designed just to lower your energy cost, but not to provide a backup. The thing is their grid-tie inverter synchronizes its voltage level and frequency with the utility. It uses the mains sinewave as a reference. When it disappears or is out of tolerance, such an inverter shuts down. There are also battery-powered solar and wind systems with special controllers that switch their operation to internal sinewave reference when grid fails. But this is not the kind of solar power systems with free installation that are advertised everywhere. In any case, they won't provide a long backup time unless you use them for the loads that consume very small amount of electricity. Therefore in this book we will cover primarily electric generators as the most common and practical backup options.

	PORTABLE GENERATOR	STANDBY GENERATOR	INVERTER WITH BATTERY	SOLAR-POWERED SYSTEM	WIND-POWERED SYSTEM
Source of stored energy	Gasoline, diesel, LPG, natural gas	Natural gas, diesel, LPG	Batteries	Batteries	Batteries
Typical Power	500-17,500 watt	6,000-20,000 watt	500-5,000 watt	2,000-5,000 watt	1,000-5,000 watt
Run time	5-10 hours	Unlimited	1-5 hours	1-5 hours	1-5 hours
Connection to your loads	Extension cords or optional transfer switch	Transfer switch	Extension cords or optional transfer relay	Direct connection of grid-tie inverter	Direct connection of grid-tie inverter
Professional installation	Optional (for transfer panel)	Required	Optional	Required	Required
Location	Outdoors	Generator-outdoors, transfer switch-indoors	Indoors	PV panels-outdoors, inverter and batteries-indoors	Turbine-outdoors, inverter and batteries-indoors
Activation	Manual	Auto	Manual or auto	Continuous operation	Continuous operation
Quality of power	Poor	Good	Excellent	Excellent	Excellent
Typical cost per kW (installed)	$100-150/ kW	$600-1200/ kW	$1,500-3,500/kW	$5,000/kW (before incentives)	$5,000/kW (before incentives)
Noise	High	Medium	Quiet	Quiet	Medium
Maintenance	Frequent	Frequent	Negligible	Negligible	Frequent
Lowering utility bill	No	No	No	Yes	Yes

Abbreviations:
kW- kilowatt (1 kW=1000 watt); LPG- liquefied propane gas

HOW GENERATORS WORK AND WHAT IS GENSET

If you are considering an electric generator you may want to have some basic understanding of its operation. By knowing how a generator works, you can be better equipped when it comes to choosing the right one for your application. So, let's first briefly review the generators operation and what is common to all of them. Technically speaking, electrical generators by definition are devices that produce electricity from mechanical energy. In the systems for residential use, the mechanical energy is provided by a rotary engine (prime mover) that drives a rotating shaft that spins an electromagnet around copper coils. The operation of such a system is based on a physical phenomenon called **electromagnetic induction**. This phenomenon is that changing the magnetic field induces a voltage in a conductor placed in this field. Particularly, if a magnetic field is spinning with a constant speed relative to a copper coil, the generated voltage in the coil is sinusoidal. The frequency of this sinusoida if determined by RPM of this rotation. Creating and changing any physical field of course requires energy. In the generator this energy is supplied by the fuel consumed by the engine. So, in practice, what we casually call a generator is actually a set consisting of the generator itself (sometimes called alternator) and an engine. These two main parts are mounted together on a common frame as a single appliance. Such a device is often referred to as engine-generator set or **genset**. In this book we will continue using the term generator even though this device contains an engine as well.

Electric generators are the most common type of backup power sources for homes. They run on a fossil-based fuel, such as natural gas, propane, diesel or gasoline. The models suitable for home use are available in a wide range from 500 watt to tens of kilowatt, so you can always find the right size for your requirements. While all residential generators have basically the same physical principles of operation, they differ by the connection, activation and fueling. We will discuss these differences in the next chapter.

YOUR OPTIONS: PORTABLE vs. STANDBY

During the infamous Northeast blackout of 2003, I heard from some people: "We should have had a generator". They tend to think about generator as if it was some kind of generic device that could provide electricity during an outage. But when they looked into various catalogs they got puzzled because they saw models ranging from $200 to $5000. Well, there is no such thing as "a" generator. There are various types of electric power generators. The two major types suitable for urban homes are portable and standby (the drawing on page 14 gives you a basic idea on how they look like). Each type obviously has its pros and cons and choosing a system usually involves a compromise between the desired level of protection and the cost. Let's go over your main options.

PORTABLE devices can be moved from place to place and are intended to be connected only when you need them. In an emergency you need to move a portable generator out of storage, fill with fuel, manually start up, and finally connect to your loads. You can run long extension cords through open doors or windows to the selected stand-alone cord-and-plug appliances (such as a refrigerator and a window a/c) that you want to power.

Gasoline and **diesel** portable models are fueled from their on-board tanks, which need to be refilled as often as several times a day if you run them continuously. If you are OK with a very short runtime (an hour or a few) a battery-based inverter system may also work for you. Both, a portable generator and an inverter can be used so to speak right out of the box and do not require any professional installation. Note that portable generators can be operated **OUTDOORS ONLY** because their engine emits carbon monoxide (just like cars). However, portable models are not weatherproof. You should store a portable generator indoors and prepare a sort of protective canopy to run it in rain or snow. Since most blackouts occur during winter, dragging a few hundred pound device out of storage through mud or snow may be challenging.

The connection via the cords is the simplest one. If you are caught off-guard by a blackout and looking for a quick solution, this is your only option. However, your built-in lights, boiler and everything else that is hardwired to your house wiring system will not be powered. If you should decide to run them too, you will need to figure out how to disconnect the required devices one by one from the building wiring and hook up to the cords (of course, you must always flip the main circuit breaker into OFF position before you do anything). This may not be an easy thing to do in a dark basement. And you would have to go through all these troubles every time you have to use a generator. If you have time, a much better and a safer solution is to install a special inlet and a device called power **transfer switch**, which we will discuss later on. A transfer switch allows you to energize selected electric circuits from a portable generator while isolating them from "dead" utility lines. An electrician can usually install it in a day, but getting a permit from your electric company may take some time. Once a transfer switch is installed, you just need to connect a portable generator to the inlet via a special generator cable and flip the transfer switch from Line to Generator.

As we mentioned, portable generators can provide power only for relatively short periods of time and require manual refueling, connection and activation. **STANDBY** (a.k.a. stationary) systems, by contrast, offer you a convenience of fully automatic operation with no refueling. Such systems include an automatic transfer panel with a control circuit. The standby generator is installed near your home and is hardwired to the transfer panel. This panel in turn is permanently connected to both the house wiring and utility lines. The generator is also hooked up to a fuel source that your house uses for heating, such as a natural gas, propane or diesel. Because all this requires professional installation, it will always take a certain amount of time until you can begin using such a system. However, once it is installed, a standby generator can be activated immediately (either manually or automatically depending on the setting you selected) and effortlessly.

It can then provide power practically indefinitely for as long as there is a flow of fuel. To be accurate, there are some more expensive portable generators can also be fueled from an external source (such as natural gas line) and can therefore provide extended run time too. However, you would still need to roll such device out from the storage, hook up to a fuel line, manually start up, and connect to your loads. A fixed system by contrast is already connected to both the house wiring and the fuel source. When it detects a power outage, it isolates your electrical wiring or designated emergency circuits from the grid, and starts up the generator. When grid voltage is restored, such a system will connect you back to the utility lines and will turn itself off. You don't even have to be at home to activate it. Note that the typical transfer time of an automatic system is 10-30 seconds. Therefore, if you run important computer applications, you may still want an UPS. It can prevent data loss during the transfer time. Also note that even though permanently installed generators can provide practically unlimited run time, you still need to periodically shut them down to change the motor oil and do other maintenance. With some types of engines you will need to do it as often as every 50-100 hours of operation. This is another reason by the way to have a supplemental UPS for your modem and computer.

It goes without saying that standby generators provide the highest level of comfort, but of course it comes with a price tag. Depending on wattage and options, a complete system with an automatic transfer switch may sell for $2000 to $5000. You will also need to spend around $4,000 to $8,000 for electrical wiring and fuel hook up. Before the installation, your contractor will need to obtain permits from your electric and fuel utilities and pass the inspections after the work is done. All this, obviously, takes certain time. So, if you are looking for an emergency generator because there is a hurricane or an ice storm in tomorrow's forecast, it is too late to consider a standby type.

WHAT GENERATOR DO I NEED?

As we discussed in the previous chapter, to buy the right system for your personal needs you have got to make several key decisions, such as:

✓ What you want to run in an emergency: a few critical appliances or entire house;
✓ For what duration of time you want to be able to use your backup source;
✓ How much money you are willing to spend.

Here is a quick selection checklist.

You should choose a **standby** home generator system if:

- Your house requires more than 17 kW power;
- You want to be prepared for long-term power outages;
- You want fully automatic operation; You don't want to move around a heavy device;
- You can spend overall $6,000-13,000 for a system and installation;
- You can wait certain time for permits and installation.

You should choose a **portable generator and a transfer switch** if:

- You are looking for a protection only against short-term outages,
- You are able to move around a few hundred pound device;
- You can wait certain time for permit and installation of transfer switch;
- You want to spend up to $2,000;
- You want to back up some hardwired appliances and to have backed up devices pre-wired.

You should choose a **portable generator without a transfer switch** if:

- You need emergency power immediately;
- You are looking for a protection only against short-term outages,
- You want to spend less than $1,500 (maybe even a few hundred dollars);
- You want to back up only a few cord-and-plug appliances via

extension cords;

- You are able to move around a few hundred pound device.

A conceptual diagram on the next page illustrates the main home generator connection options, which we will discuss below.

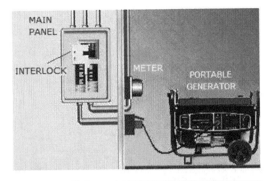

PORTABLE GENERATOR WITH MECHANICAL INTERLOCK AND ADDITIONAL DOUBLE-BREAKER IN MAIN PANEL

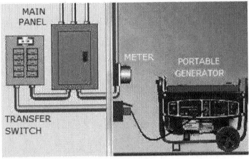

PORTABLE GENERATOR WITH ADDITIONAL SUBPANEL

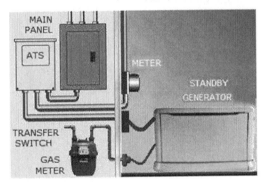

WHOLE HOUSE STANDBY GENERATOR WITH AUTOMATIC TRANSFER SWITCH

Conceptual diagrams of generator connection for various configurations.
Generator exhaust should be facing away from the building. Spacing should comply with NFPA 37 and local codes (typically >10 ft for portable and >5 ft. for standby). The drawing is not to scale.

PORTABLE GENERATORS

Portable electrical generators are designed to temporarily provide AC power by burning supplied fuels. As the name implies, these devices are intended for stand-alone (non-hardwired) applications. Homeowners normally use them to energize a few appliances, although high-end portable models can power an entire house. The connection can be made via extension cords or via a pre-installed transfer switch. Besides home use, portable generators are utilized on construction sites, farms, motor homes, recreation vehicles, in camping trips, and basically everywhere where the grid is not available. Currently, they are available in the range of 500W to 20kW, which will fit most homeowners' requirements. Their main advantages are they are generally cheaper than standby systems and may be used right away without the need of a professional installation.

CHOOSING THE FUEL

People sometimes tend to think about a generator as if it is a kind of generic device. In reality, it comes in various types, which we are going to discuss below. Depending on the design, generator engine can run on gasoline, diesel, propane, or natural gas. Not surprisingly, each design has its advantages and disadvantages. So, let's go over each type and outline its pros and cons.

Gasoline and **diesel** models are powered from the on-board tank- this is what makes these generators truly portable. Unfortunately, these models have short run time- typically it is less than twelve hours per tankful. If you run such a device continuously at rated load you will need to shut it down several times a day for refueling. There are more expensive models that can be hooked up to an external fuel source (natural gas, LPG or diesel) and supply electricity for extended periods of time. They can be used as portable home generators. Gasoline-powered devices generally cost less than all other types. You can buy for example a basic 4000 watt gas model for about $300. If you go by price alone, it may be a good choice. However this type has a major often ignored disadvantage: when the grid is down or after a major natural disaster the gasoline may not be available. During the widespread Northeast blackout of 2003 in entire East coast gas pumps did not work for three days. After Superstorm Sandy of 2012 I had to wait four hours on line to get gas. To assure backup electricity during an unexpected wide-spread blackout you would need to store at home a substantial supply of gasoline. Gasoline fumes are highly flammable, which makes storing of large amount of gas unsafe. Note that unleaded gasoline has a relatively short shelf life- it can begin breaking down in about six months and may gum up the fuel system. Manufacturers of some stabilizers claim their products can extend gas shelf life to two years. Assuming this is true, you would need to recycle your emergency supply at least every other year. Also note that a gasoline engine requires frequent maintenance, such as periodic oil changes as often as every 20 hours or so. If not properly maintained, it may have startup problems especially at cold weather due to gum deposits.

Diesel generators are the most efficient, more quite, have the longest engine's life, but generally are also the most expensive. Diesel is the least flammable fuel source and has longer shelf line, but it likewise may not be available during a blackout.

Liquefied propane gas or **LPG** (casually cold propane) can be easily stored in both small and large tanks, has practically unlimited shelf life, and besides natural gas is the only fuel that may be available during major power interruptions. That's why I believe LPG SHOULD BE YOUR FIRST CHOICE for portable emergency power. By the way, among all types, LPG-powered generator will more likely start in extremely cold weather.

Multi-fuel portable generators offer more options when one type of fuel is not available. Some models can run on natural gas, gasoline and propane. A simple adjustment is needed to switch from one fuel to another. If you made a natural gas hook up outdoors, you could use such a generator for a long period of time without worrying about refueling. Unfortunately, tri-fuel devices may cost 100% more than single-fuel gasoline ones. More practical are bi-fuel models that run on LPG (propane) and gasoline. There are good bi-fuel models that don't cost much more than regular ones, such as mid-sized Westighouse WGEN 7500.

COMPARING THE MODELS

The chart in the next page compares the main characteristics and typical cost of some popular models. We can see that Predator generator sold by Harbor Freight Tools has the lowest cost per watt among compared mid-sized models. You will have to pay some extra if you want a wheel kit though. Another Predator model 68530 was on the 2014 "best buy" list of a leading consumer magazine. Of course, price is not the only thing. In their later review they awarded best buy ratings to Generac RS7000E, Troy-Bilt® XP7000 30477, and Generac GP5500 5939. However, the consumer magazine tested only gasoline portable models. What would they do with a best-rated gasoline-fueled device when gas pumps run dry or don't have power? In my view the best buy is dual fuel Westinghouse WGEN 7500DF. With wheel kit, fuel gauge and remote start, it has everything you would want at a reasonable price,

Notes: In our chart the run time for gasoline and diesel generators is given per tankful; for propane generators- per 20-lb tank. Prices represent the best numbers we found online at the time we compiled this review (last updated March 2018). Of course, the prices usually fluctuate and can vary from place to place. Unfortunately, after a hurricane or a major storm, discount online retailers usually run out of stock, and generator prices are spiking.

Brand	Model	Rated kW	Surge kW	Fuel	Electric start	Run time @50% load	Typ. price ($)	$ per kW
Generac	5735 GP17500	17.5	26.2	Gas	yes	10 hr.	2999	171
Generac	5802 XG10000E	10	12.5	Gas	yes	10 hr.	2000	200
Westinghouse	WGEN 7500DF	7.5/ 6.75	9.5/ 8.5	Gas/ LPG	yes	11 hr.	950	127
Champion	100165	7.5	9.375	Gas/ LPG	yes	8 hr./ 5.5 hr.	950	127
Briggs & Stratton	30663	7	8.75	Gas	yes	9 hr.	990	141
Predator	63085	7	8.75	Gas	yes	12 hr.	600	86
Generac	6673	7	8.75	Gas	yes	10 hr.	950	136
Ridgid	RD906812	6.8	8.5	Gas	no	12 hr.	1550	228
Sportsman	GEN7000LP	6	7	LPG	yes	8 hr	800	133
Pulsar	PG7000D	5.5	7	Diesel	yes	11 hr.	1800	327
Honda	EU7000iS	5.5	7	Gas	yes	10 hr.	4000	727
Generac	GP5500 5939	5.5	6.8	Gas	no	10 hr.	690	125
Duromax	XP4850EH	3.85	4.85	Gas/ LPG	yes	12 hr./ 16 hr.	400	123
DuroStar	DS4000S	3.3	4	Gas	no	8 hr.	280	85

Abbreviations:
kW- kilowatt (1kW=1,000 watt); LPG- liquefied propane gas.

FEATURES and OPTIONS

When choosing a portable generator, aside from reliability, rated wattage, fuel type and price, there are a number of other features and accessories to consider. Most generators will sound like a lawn mower. So-called quiet models are still noisy, although to a lesser degree, and obviously they cost more. If you consider a portable generator, you may want to check if there are any noise restrictions in your neighborhood. Besides lower noise, look for the following useful features: voltage regulator (AVR), electric start (in addition to manual recoil), OHV engine, twist-lock receptacles, and oil gauge. If you plan to use your device without a transfer switch, look for a built-in GFCI for additional safety. Many models have all of the above.

Another useful feature is a **fuel gauge**. Here is why. All operation manuals tell you to disconnect loads before shutting down the generator. You should never let your genset run out of fuel while being loaded. When an engine runs out of gas or propane pressure drops too low, the RPF and output voltage can vary widely before the genset shuts down. During this time you can damage your connected motor-driven appliances (like a refrigerator) or damage the generator's AVR. That's why a gas level meter is very handy. Unfortunately, I am not aware of any model that lets you watch propane pressure.

Since a typical model may weight several hundred pounds, you may want to get a wheel kit- devices with wheels can be moved around by one person. If you want a quieter operation or a clean sinusoidal voltage for sensitive electronics, you may consider **inverter-generators**. An inverter-generator in addition to an engine and an alternator includes a solid-state rectifier and an electronic DC-AC converter integrated into a single appliance. Such a device produces a clean sinewave with THD below 3%, although cheaper models may produce a modified sinewave. Their engine does not have to run at full speed constantly. It automatically adjusts speed depending on the electrical demand. All this makes it more fuel efficient and much quieter. Another advantage of inverter generators is some models can be paralleled for higher power. Note that you can't just connect them together- you need to buy an optional parallel adapter that forces two devices to synchronize their operation. Unfortunately, inverter-generators are typically priced twice as high as regular ones.

NOISE CONSIDERATIONS

A portable generator may be as loud as a lawn mower, which is something you need to take into consideration. Most places have local noise ordinances, which set the allowable sound level that can cross property lines. For example, in U.S. the typical numbers for continuous noise in residential urban areas are 57 dBA daytime and 47 dBA nighttime, although it's possible that during an emergency these restrictions may be waived or ignored.

Let me first quickly explain how sound is measured. Noise levels are usually measured in decibel (dB). Since human ear has different sensitivity to different frequencies, the noise levels are often measured with a so-called A-filter whose frequency response is similar to that of our ear. These frequency-weighting results are stated in dB(A) or dBA. Here are typical dBA levels associated with various sources:

Gas lawn mower at 3 ft. – 90-100;
Heavy street traffic at 15 ft. – 85;
TV at moderate volume 65;
Normal conversation – 60;
Library – 35.

Sound levels depend on the distance from the source. For example, every time the distance doubles, the pressure level decreases by half, i.e. by 6 dB. It is customary to measure a generator sound at 7 meters (23 feet) distance. But in general, there is no industry standard way for testing decibel ratings on portable generators. Many major manufacturers do not even list the decibels of their models. Some provide dB without specifying at what power level they are obtained. All this makes it hard to compare different brands.

Generally, inverter generators are the quietest ones among the portables. Their typical noise level at rated load is 60 to 65 dBA. Regular portable generators may have 65 to 70 dBA. If noise level is critical to you, you should choose an inverter- generator. Yamaha (such as EF2000iS) and Honda (such as EU2000i) are among the quietest brands in this category. However, they are also among the most expensive ones. Some imports such as Champion's 73536i may also be sufficiently quiet for half of the cost of top ranking domestic and Japanese ones. Besides lower noise, inverter generators have lower fuel consumption and better quality of power. Not surprisingly, they typically cost 2 to 5 times more than conventional models. The chart compares characteristics of some quiet generators.

Manufacturer and model	dBA at 1/4 load	dBA at 100% load	Typical Price
Yamaha EF2000iS	51.5	61	$950
Hyundai HY2000si	-	65	$670
Powerhouse PH2100PRi	56	66	$660
Champion 73536i	53	65	$380
Honda EU2000i	53	59	$1000

HOW TO CONNECT

The simplest method of hooking up your AC loads to a portable generator is by using extension cords. The generator control panel has several standard 120V outlets. You can just plug 3-wire cables into these outlets and run them through open doors or windows to the appliances you want to power. Be sure to use heavy duty outdoor-rated cords. The required wire size depends on its length and the rated load current. As a rule of thumb, #12 AWG cord is sufficient for currents up to 20 A. Models rated above 5 kW usually also provide at least one 120/240 output via their 30 or 50 amp 4-hole twist-lock receptacle. With such a receptacle, instead of running individual cables, you may use a special 4-wire generator cord with several outlets on the load end.

The method with the cords perhaps is your only option if you are looking for a quick solution. However your lights and everything else that is directly connected to your house wiring will not be powered. You will need to figure out how to disconnect them one by one from the building wiring and then connect to the cords. You would have to go through all these troubles every time you need to use a generator. This is something many people don't realize beforehand. A more convenient and safe method is to hook up your power source to the house via a pre-wired **transfer switch**. It connects your house either to the generator or to the grid and prevents so-called **backfeeding**. Backfeeding can hurt anyone working on the power line or coming in contact with a wire and is illegal. A transfer switch also protects your generator from damage if the service restores while it is running. We will discuss different types of transfer switches in the next chapter. Once you wired the switch, all you need to do is roll out your generator from storage and connect its high-current twist-lock receptacle to the inlet box via a single generator cable. You can either buy such a ready-to-use cable or you can get proper plug and a socket and build it by yourself. Below you will find pinout diagrams of the common generator outlets. The hook-up via a transfer switch is safer and gives you more flexibility. However, obviously, it increases your cost and requires a professional installation. Also note, most guides and reviews won't tell you that a generator with GFCI will not work with a regular transfer panel. See page 31 for more details and workaround. If in an emergency you really must connect a generator to a building wiring without a transfer switch, the most important thing to remember is that the main service disconnect should be flipped to the "OFF" position prior to connecting the generator. Be sure to turn the main circuit breaker off before you connect a generator, and disconnect generator before turning the service back on. If you accidentally do not follow the "proper sequence", you will be backfeeding. The following chapters will discuss various transfer system options.

CONNECTORS AND PINOUTS

In addition to conventional 120V outlets, control panel of a portable generator usually has one or several different high-current receptacles. The generic standard for AC power connectors in North America is ANSI/NEMA WD 6-2012. It defines as much as 150 different styles. That's why wiring the plugs or cords may be confusing. Fortunately, only a handful of outlet types are practically used in portable generators.

The chart below provides wiring configurations of common single-phase generator outlets. The ampacity of the largest outlet determines the amount of power you can get via a transfer switch. For example, 50-amp NEMA 14-50 would provide up to $240V \times 50A = 12,000$ volt-amps. If you generator is rated above 12kW, for the balance of the power you need to run extension cords.

CONNECTOR DESCRIPTION	NEMA P/N	WIRE SIZE (AWG)	DIAGRAM
Three-pole 120/240V - 20A locking	L14-20	12	W X Y G
Two-pole 120V - 30A locking	L5-30	10	W G X
Three-pole 120/240V - 30A locking	L14-30	10	X G W Y
Two-pole 120V - 30A RV style	TT-30 (RV30)	10	W X G
Three-pole 120/240V - 50A non-locking	14-50	6	W X Y G

X and Y- electrically "hot" wires (usually red and black); W- neutral (white); G- ground (green)

PORTABLE GENERATORS SAFETY

Your owner's manual of course will include the recommended safety rules. Nevertheless, I want to emphasize certain basic things because many people tend to skip safety pages in the manuals.

- Just like all engine containing devices, electric generators should always be used **OUTDOORS**. You should locate them at least 10 feet away from the house with exhaust facing away from door and windows to avoid carbon monoxide and fumes build up.
- A generator should never be connected directly into a wall outlet or your house wiring unless it is isolated from the service lines.
- You should never add fuel while portable generator is running. To add fuel or change oil you should shut down the generator and wait until its surfaces cool down.
- Do not fill fuel tank to the top. Leave some room for the fuel to expand;
- For a safety and peace of mind it is preferable to have a model that is listed with the Underwriter's Laboratory (UL) or FM, or a respective safety agency in your country.
- You should have Carbon Monoxide (CO) and smoke detectors indoors in operating condition. In many states it is actually required by law.

The above list of course is not intended to substitute or replace official codes, standards and operation manual.

LESSER KNOWN FACTS

Advertised features of portable generators may be confusing or even misleading to the consumers. Here are some important lesser-known things to know.

- Nameplate or advertised wattage usually represents surge (starting) watts. The running watts can be 65-80% of the nameplate value. For example, if a device is listed as (say) 5,000 watt, in reality it may continuously provide only some 3,500-4,000 watt;
- Runtime is normally specified at half-load;
- The stated warranty is for consumer use. The warranty for commercial applications (if any) may be much shorter. If you

are going to use a device at a job site, read fine print;

- If your model has electric start, you will need to buy a starting battery and a charger. Most models do not include them;
- If a generator has GFCI (GFI), it will not work with a regular double-pole transfer switch without a modification because the neutral will be grounded in two places;
- You should always disconnect your loads before shutting down a portable generator. When it starts running out of fuel, RPM and frequency will fluctuate, which may damage your generator or connected devices.

CONNECTING A PORTABLE GENERATOR TO HOUSE WIRING

When you supply electricity to the home from any external source, the main thing to remember is you must avoid exporting power back into the grid. This is called **backfeeding** or islanding. It is illegal and dangerous because it creates high voltage in a small portion ("island") of the electrical network and endangers utility workers and your neighbors who think the lines are "dead". Therefore you need an additional device that can safely connect your house wiring either to the utility lines, or to your generator, but never to both at the same time. Such a device is called power **TRANSFER SWITCH**. It comes in two flavors- manual and automatic. Automatic switches are normally used with standby (permanent) generator systems. They are either included in the system or the generator manufacturer provides you with a few recommended choices to pick from. Manual switches are normally used with portable generators, but they can be used with standby systems as well. Note that there is a special class of devices called grid-tied (a.k.a. utility-interactive) inverters that can operate parallel to the utility. They don't need an external transfer switch: they synchronize their operation with the utility voltage and when grid fails, their internal contactor automatically isolates the inverter output from the service lines. But inverters are not generators- they run off a battery and produce voltage by using semiconductor devices.

There are different types of manual switches to choose from. Below we will tell you what types are available, will explain their pros and cons, and will help you choose the right one depending on your requirements.

120V or 240V: UNDERSTANDING THE HOME WIRING SYSTEM

Before discussing the types of transfer switches, let's first quickly review the configuration of home electrical wiring and explain how it affects the connection and sizing of your system. Most homes in U.S. have 3-wire 120/240V service. In essence, there are two separate 120V lines with common neutral connected to two bus bars in your main electric panel. Throughout the house some of the wall outlets are connected to Line 1, other- to Line 2. Large appliances such as a central a/c or a dryer normally run off 240V and therefore draw current from both lines (see a conceptual diagram on page 39). House wiring also includes a ground wire, but it is used for safety and under normal conditions does not carry any current. If you want to be able to energize your entire house wiring (via a transfer switch of course), you need a power source providing dual 120V/240V. Most mid to high-power portable generators as well as all home standby generators do provide 120V/240V. Most commercially available inverters for residential application provide only 120V, but they often have an option of "stacking" two devices together for 240V. Small portable generators (under 4000 watt) usually provide only 120V and therefore can't be used to energize your house wiring.

INTERLOCK KIT

This is the cheapest way to safely retrofit transfer equipment into your existing electrical box. The mechanical interlock is basically a system of slide plates. It ensures that the main service breaker and a generator breaker cannot be activated at the same time. Depending on the brand and type, the interlock kit can cost from as low as $20 to $100 (of course you need to pick the one that is compatible with your breakers and panel). You will also need to install an additional double-pole breaker for the generator line, and an outdoor inlet for connecting your generator. These connections have to be done by a licensed electrician and it may cost several hundred to one thousand dollars plus possibly the cost of a permit. Once everything is installed, you can easily switch from utility to a generator. The basic transfer procedure will be as follows:

- Start up the generator and let it warm up for several minutes. At this point it is still isolated from your home;
- Turn off main service breaker and off all individual breakers;
- Slide interlock plate;
- Connect your generator to the inlet by using a generator cord (see the diagrams of different connectors);
- Turn on the generator breaker;
- Start turning on needed individual breakers one a time while making sure you don't overload the generator.

To switch back to the service you will have to reverse the above procedure. Here are the main advantages and disadvantages of an interlock kit.

INTERLOCK PROS:

- Lowest cost;
- Allows emergency power to the whole house;
- Does not require re-wiring of your existing circuits. You just need to install a dual generator breaker and wire it to an outdoor inlet.

INTERLOCK CONS:

- You need 2 or 3 available slots in your load box right below the existing main breaker.
- You will have to relocate the existing branch circuits from these positions;
- Some interlock models may also interfere with adjacent slots;
- Some kits will not function when the cover is removed;
- If you do not have enough free spaces in your breaker box, you will need to add so-called piggyback breakers for missing spaces;

- You need to use only an interlock designed for the brand of your existing load center;
- You may easily overload your generator if you don't know exactly how much current each circuit consumes (this is a common drawback of all whole-house transfer switches).

TRANSFER SWITCH FOR ENTIRE SERVICE

In older electrical systems the main service disconnect and individual breakers are located in separate panels. With this configuration or if for any reason your breaker panel does not allow installation of an extra double-pole switch, you can install a separate box with a manual transfer switch. Note that in practice, what is advertised as a manual transfer switch is actually a system that has two double-pole switches and a locking mechanism that prevents both switches from being activated at the same time. You need to manually operate this mechanism to switch from utility to a generator. If you go for this option, you can buy a single-load switch, such as Generac p/n 6333 for around a $100. Your installer will need to break the connection between the service disconnect and existing distribution box and install this switch in between. If your portable generator is not big enough for the whole house, which is usually the case, in an emergency you will need to keep some breakers in OFF position leaving only those branches you want to energize. Such an option costs a bit more than an interlock kit and requires more re-wiring work. Just like with an interlock, you may easily overload your generator if you don't know exactly how much current each circuit consumes.

The general procedure of activating backup power via a single-load transfer panel during a blackout is as follows:
- Turn off all individual breakers in the main panel;
- Start up your generator outdoors and connect it to the inlet via a generator cord (at this point the generator is still isolated and is just warming up);
- Move the switch in the transfer panel from "Line" to "Generator" position.

- If by this time your generator has warmed up, begin turning on individual breakers in the distribution panel one at a time while making sure you don't overload the generator.

Unless you previously determined electric currents in all circuits you plan to activate, it is very easy to overload the generator. If you are not sure about the actual value of your electric loads, you may want to monitor electric currents in both lines L1 and L2 while you are turning on the breakers. If you have a proper electrical training and know how to safely work with electricity, you can do it by yourself. All you need is a hand-held clamp-on amp meter and line-worker's rubber gloves. To do the measurement wear rubber gloves, remove front panel of the breaker box and enclose within the clamp-on device each "hot" line cable (usually red and black) one at a time. You don't have to do the measurement in the neutral cable.

A SUB-PANEL FOR ESSENTIAL LINES

This option is the most convenient though it is more expensive (installation of a sub-panel may cost around $1,000). You will have a separate box that includes both interlocked switches and individual breakers for your selected lines. It makes sense to choose this option if you don't want to deal with finding in dark basement the breakers you want to activate and risking overloading your generator. You can pick in advance the lines you want to backup making sure your generator can handle them and have your electrician relocate these lines from your main distribution box to the sub-panel. He will also need to wire the sub-panel to additional two-pole breaker that will protect the sub-panel and install an outdoor inlet. During normal operation your essential loads will pass through the transfer panel, while the remaining ones will be fed directly from the main box. The diagram below shows an example of wiring of a sub-panel.

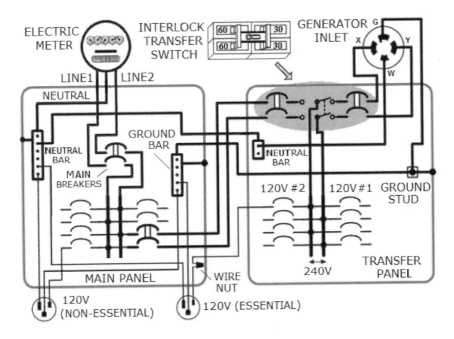

With this method, the general procedure of activating backup power during a blackout is as follows:

- Toggle "Line" switch in the sub-panel to "OFF" position and turn off all individual breakers;
- Start up your generator outdoors and connect its twist-lock outlet to the inlet via a generator cord (at this point the generator is still isolated and is just warming up);
- Slide the interlock plate and flip the "generator breaker" to "ON" position.
- If by this time your generator has warmed up, begin turning on individual breakers in the transfer sub-panel one at a time.

The branches left in the main load box will not be energized during a blackout. When the service is restored, the lights and devices connected to those lines will turn on, alerting you that the grid is back. Note that since the loads which are using backup power are isolated from the mains, there will be no danger of back feeding. You will just need to turn off the breakers in the sub-panel and then flip the transfer switch back to "LINE" and shut down your generator. When you do this, there will be a brief interruption of power on transfer pane lines.

Note that some consumer guides incorrectly state that with a separate transfer panel you can leave all your branch circuits "ON" when you are starting up the generator. This is wrong because the initial surge currents of your motor-driven appliances and lights may overload the generator and trip its overcurrent protection. You do want to power up your loads one at a time to let generator stabilize after each additional load.

GENERLINK™

This is a special brand of redundant equipment. It looks like a collar that is inserted behind your electric meter. During a blackout you will need to plug your portable generator to the GenerLink™ inlet and start it up. After that the system automatically switches your house from the mains to your generator. While sometimes this system is advertised as automatic, it is actually semi-automatic: you still need to manually connect and start up the generator. Since the installation requires breaking the meter's seal, it is normally done by a local utility. The system may cost $500 to $1,000 installed. Some utilities may install GenerLink™ for free and charge certain monthly service fee instead. Since this system transfers entire service, it has the same disadvantage as all whole house transfer systems. To avoid overloading your generator you will need to turn off all breakers before starting up the generator and turn on only some of them one at a time while making sure you don't exceed the generator capacity.

AN ISSUE WITH GFCI

Many portable generators are equipped with so-called Ground Fault Circuit Interrupt (GFCI), a.k.a Ground Fault Interrupter (GFI) to meet OSHA requirements for construction sites. When you are trying to connect such a generator to a transfer switch, GFCI will trip and no outlet will function. Below I'll explain you the issue and will describe the solutions.

WHAT DOES GFCI DO? GFCI is intended to protect

people from electric shocks. When it detects a hazardous current to earth ground that can flow through a human body, it opens the circuit. Some GFCI can also detect ground to neutral faults. There are various designs of these devices, but they all have one thing in common: a current sense transformer wound on a high permeability core. Its primary is made by passing all line and neutral wires through the center of this core. The secondary coil is used as a sense coil.

Under normal conditions the sum of currents leaving the outlet equals to the sum of return currents, and the net current through the core is zero. If a person gets into a contact with an electric wire (L1 or L2), a portion of current will flow to ground through the body. This will cause current imbalance in the GFCI transformer, which in turn will create current in the sense coil. The control circuit will detect this condition and trip the main circuit breaker (typically within 25 milliseconds). The GFCI trip threshold usually is set as low as $\pm$ 5mA, so it is supposed to de-energize the outlets before serious shock occurs.

WHY IS GFCI TRIPPING WITH TRANSFER SWITCH?

In generators equipped with GFCI, the frame is bonded to neutral (otherwise, GFCI would not function). In the transfer switch the neutral is also bonded to ground. As the result, a portion of neutral current flows through the ground lead of the generator cable, which causes an imbalance of GFCI transformer, which treats it as a fault. To fix this problem you need to remove second ground connection of generator's neutral, i.e. to make neutral grounded only in one place. This can be accomplished in a number of ways.

SOLUTIONS TO GFCI PROBLEM:

Option 1. Open generator cover and remove neutral bond jumper wire. This disables GFCI. Attach a label stating "Neutral Unbonded". If later on you will need to use this generator elsewhere without a transfer switch, you should re-install the neutral bond before use, since it is not safe to operate it without GFCI.

Option 2. Inside your transfer switch lift the ground wire coming from generator inlet (isolate the loose end). Your genset will still be grounded via its neutral wire in generator cord. Attach a label stating "Ground Disconnected". If you later will need to connect a different generator without bonded neutral, you will need to re-connect the ground wire in transfer switch before use.

Option 3. Install Switched Neutral Kit (such as Generac model 6297 that sells for under $100), which can upgrade most manual transfer switches from continuous neutral to switched neutral. When the transfer switch is in GEN mode, the kit disconnects generator's neutral from utility.

Option 4. Install a 3-pole (neutral switching) transfer switch, such as Eaton CH10GEN503 that sells for about $400.

For the above Options 3 and 4 the installation just like any wiring should be done by a licensed professional.

STANDBY GENERATORS

Standby (a.k.a. stationary or fixed) systems are permanently connected to your house wiring via a transfer system and hooked up to a fuel source. Normally this would be the same source you already use for the heating: natural gas, propane or diesel. All fixed power systems include three main parts: an engine-generator set (genset), a transfer panel, and a control circuit. The generator is always mounted outdoors. It has to be hardwired to a transfer panel and connected to a fuel line. The transfer panel is normally installed indoors. The control circuit is continuously monitoring the condition of the mains voltage. If the utility power is down or its voltage drops below a preset level, the control circuit starts up the generator. First it lets it warm up for certain time, typically from 5 seconds to one minute. Then it disconnects your house from utility lines and connects it to the generator. During the transfer time the device is powered from an external battery.

Normally, a stationary generator is mounted on a cement pad. It should be located preferably near the fuel source. Many models already come with a mounting pad. However, you still need to prepare a flat location that has provisions for water drainage. A little tip: due to the heavy weight, you may want to request lift gate service when the freight company calls you for the delivery. Otherwise, have at least four strong persons present to unload the device. To prevent exhaust gases from entering the house, the unit should be located in a well-ventilated area with exhaust away from doors or windows. The installation should comply with the National Fire Protection Association (NFPA) standard NFPA 37 and local codes. NFPA 37 particularly requires at least 5 ft. (1.5 m) minimum clearance between exhaust of standby generator weatherproof enclosure and any structure, shrubs, trees, etc.

YOUR CONNECTION OPTIONS

There are two main stationary system configurations.

Option 1. WHOLE HOUSE GENERATOR

If wattage of the model you picked is sufficient to power the whole house and you have the main service disconnect in a separate panel, you can have a transfer system installed between the main disconnect and your existing circuit panel. You transfer switch should have the same or greater amperage as compared to the main circuit breaker. With this setup, you don't have to re-wire individual branches since you will be switching the entire service.

Option 2. PARTIAL HOUSE GENERATOR

If you chose a system that is not large enough to run the whole house, you will need a sub-panel for critical lines which you want to be energized in an emergency. Automatic transfer systems often come with a built-in sub-panel. Your electrician will need to re-wire the selected circuits from the existing breaker box to this sub-panel. With the first option, you pay more for a larger generator, but you save on the installation costs since you don't have to move individual circuits. With the second option, you save on the cost of the generator, but pay extra for the labor. Nowadays many automatic models come with a so-called digital load management (DLM) control. This technology lets you prioritize your appliances. If your system approaches its maximum capacity, the DLM starts shedding less important loads to prevent generator overload. This option allows you to buy a smaller generator.

WHAT MODEL TO CHOOSE

There are a number of generator brands available on the market. The main U.S. manufacturers of standby systems are Generac®, Kohler, Briggs & Stratton, and Cummins® Onan®. As far as I know, Siemens, Eaton and Honeywell models were actually made by Generac. Likewise, GE and Milbank were made by Briggs & Stratton.

Apparently, private label arrangements did not work well because most of these "brands" discontinued. Generac is the largest U.S. manufacturer of home generators: its market share used to be greater than 70%. It offers a broad selection of residential stationary systems in the power range from 6kW to 22kW. Generac Guardian® series seems to be on the low end of the price range. The published characteristics of all main brands are quite similar. Kohler claims the fastest transfer time- its units restore power within 10 seconds of an outage. Most domestic brands these days provide from 3 to 5 years of limited warranty. Of course, as the name implies, these warranties have some limitations- refer to official documents for complete information. Particularly, advertised warranty is only for residential use. Commercial warranty (if any) is usually much shorter-- read fine print.

Most standby generators have either steel or aluminum enclosures. Steel normally costs less. If you live in a salt air coastal area, and you are concerned of enclosure's corrosion, you may want an aluminum enclosure, which typically adds a few hundred dollars to the cost. Other than that, for a given power requirement, among top American brands, I would just use price as the main selection criterion (see for example my picks on page 53). The chart on the next page compares main characteristics and prices of some popular models. I compiled this chart to save you time from going through all the datasheet. As far as we can see, cost wise in the range 15-20 kW the Generac line has lowest dollar per watt ratio, and in my view is the first choice.

Brand	Model	Rated power (kW) NG/LPG	Fuel rate (CHF) NG/LPG	Case	Typ. price	$ per kw (NG)
Generac	7039	20/18	301/130	Aluminum	$4,600	230
Briggs & Stratton	40395	18/20	260/135	Steel	$4,400	244
Generac	7036	16/16	309/107	Aluminum	$3,775	236
Cummins® Onan®	RS13A + A045P692	11/13	253/85	Aluminum	$2,950 +$380	256
Kohler®	14RESAL	12/14	193/87	Composite	$3,725	333
Briggs & Stratton	40445	6/8	94/37.8	Steel	$2,000	317
Generac	6898 PowerPact	6/7.5	117/52	Steel	$1,880	313

Abbreviations: kW- kilowatt (1 kW=1000 watt); NG- natural gas; LPG- liquefied propane gas; CFH- cubic feet per hour.

Note: Prices represent the best numbers we found online at the time we compiled this review. Of course, the prices fluctuate, vary from place to place, an usually surge after a major natural disaster. At the risk of stating the obvious, check the current prices before you buy.

IS YOUR NATURAL GAS SERVICE SUFFICIENT?

Before choosing a particular natural gas generator, you need to make sure your gas service is sufficient to run this system. The residential customers normally get depressurized gas delivered via small pipes (0.5-1.5"), called "services". The household appliances are typically designed to operate at 0.1-0.2 psi and normally include a regulator to drop the incoming line pressure to this level. Natural gas pressure at many homes served by old lines is 0.2-0.3 psi. Newer service lines may operate at 2-50 psi. For these systems, the gas meter includes a regulator that reduces the incoming pressure to 0.2-0.25 psi. Most home generators are designed to work from standard gas pressure 0.18-0.25 psi (5 to 7 inches of water column), so you should not have problem with this. However, occasionally some high power models may need a higher pressure. A bigger issue may be with the natural gas **flow rate**. To produce its rated power a generator needs certain amount of fuel. It is usually specified in cubic feet per hour (CFH). Our chart above provides the published number for each model. We can see for example, that an 18kW natural gas generator (which is a model advertised as 20kW based on its propane rating) needs about 260 CFH. Most residential gas meters are rated only 250 CFH or less. You can find the capacity of your existing meter on its nameplate label. It is stated either in CFH or Btu/hour (1 CFH≈1000 Btu/h).

When you assess your gas requirements don't forget that you also need to run furnaces and other gas appliances. To run a large standby generator you will likely need to ask your gas company to upgrade your service. They can install a larger high-flow meter or a second meter. Your utility may charge you anywhere from $100 to $5,000 to upgrade your meter- call them up to find out their fees. Some may waive the charge if you are also installing a standard appliance that needs high gas flow rate. If the cost turns out to be too high, you may want to choose a smaller genset- for example a 6 kW model requires less than 100 CFH.

LESSER KNOWN FACTS

- The advertised rating of most dual-fuel standby models is for operation on propane. Maximum power with natural gas is typically 5-10% lower. Our chart above provides wattage both for propane and natural gas;
- Rated power is usually given for 60 $^{\circ}$F (15.5 $^{\circ}$C) ambient at sea level. In summer and at higher elevations the available output will be lower. You need to derate available watts typically 3.5% for each 1000 ft. (305 m) above sea level and 1.5% for each 10 $^{\circ}$F (12.5 $^{\circ}$C) rise in ambient temperature above 60 $^{\circ}$F. For example, a 15 kW device would provide only about 14.1 kW at 100 $^{\circ}$F.
- All automatic systems require a battery which usually is not included in the set;
- Advertised warranty is for residential use. Read fine print for commercial warranty (if any).

SIZING A BACKUP GENERATOR FOR HOME USE

Practically all domestic manufacturers of generators and many retailers provide sizing guides with the wattage charts or load calculators. However, in my view, most of them are not very helpful for two reasons:

- Actual wattage of your particular appliance obviously depends on its make, size, and year of manufacturing and may differ significantly from the average numbers provided in these guides;
- Most sizing guides don't take into account possible imbalance of the electric load in your home electrical system. Required size of the emergency power system depends not only on your total power need but also on the system configuration and wiring as we will explain below.

SIZING A WHOLE HOUSE GENERATOR

If you have a standard in North America 3-wire 120/240V electric service, you basically have two separate 120V buses (let's call them lines L1 and L2) as explained on the page 25. Most cord-and-plug devices, such as room a/c, stove, refrigerators, as well as lights are 120V devices, so they draw current only from one of two lines. Since their location and the choice of outlets throughout the house are pretty much random, two 120V lines in the house wiring in most cases are imbalanced. A home generator likewise has two 120V outputs with common neutral, each of which can supply not more than half of the generator total rated wattage. For example, in an 8,000 watt 120/240V generator, each 120V bus can provide only 4,000 watt. Therefore, if you are looking for a whole house backup system, it's not enough to find out your house lump power consumption as many sizing guides suggest-- this would be a common mistake. You need to know how the electric load is split between two lines. Note that this is not an issue in Europe and other places with 2-wire electrical service.

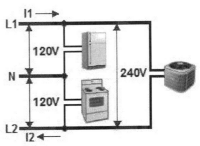

HOME WIRING SYSTEM HAS TWO 120V LINES WITH COMMON NEUTRAL

TO SIZE A GENSET, MEASURE I1 AND I2 AND MULTIPLY THE GREATEST OF THESE TWO BY 240

Let me illustrate it with the following example. Suppose your house needs 8kW power. If this consumption splits equally between L1 and L2, in theory you could use an 8kW generator. However, if your appliances consume for example 6 kW from L1 and 2 kW from L2, you would need an emergency system capable of supplying 6 kW from its both 120V outputs, which would be a 12 kW system. That's why for a whole house backup system, you need to determine the distribution of electric load in your home. You may ask your electrician to measure electric currents on L1 and L2 with a clamp-on multimeter while all your appliances are operating. Then multiply the greater of these two values by 240V. In Europe and other places with a 2-wire system you would need to measure current only on one of 2 lines and multiply it by the voltage.

SIZING PROCEDURE

1. Turn on all devices and lights that you want to operate in an

emergency and measure continuous electric currents (I1 and I2) on both lines L1 and L2 as described above.

2. Take the largest of I1 or I2 and multiply it by 240. This will be your required wattage.

Example. Suppose your measurements on the two lines are I1=30A and I2=20A. You need a generator that can provide at least 30A from each of its outputs. In this case, you need one rated for 30A×240V=7,200 watt. If you found a substantial imbalance of L1, L2 loads, you may want to have your electrician swap some circuit breakers. In our example, if the loads were balanced they would be 25A each and you would need 25×240=6,000 W generator instead of 7,200 W. If you have a central air conditioner or another large motor-driven appliance, see the section on starting a central a/c.

SIZING A PARTIAL HOUSE GENERATOR

When you choose to backup only certain selected circuits in your house, these circuits will have to be disconnected from the breakers in your existing main distribution panel and routed to an additional panel called sub-panel. This sub-panel likewise has two bus bars that will be powered by two 120V outputs of backup generator. Therefore the sizing procedure should be the same as above for a whole house system, except you would need to measure electric loads on two 120V lines that go to sub-panel rather than the main panel. Once you measured electric currents on both lines going to sub-panel, take the larger one and multiply it by 240. The product will yield your required wattage.

SIZING A GENERATOR TO START CENTRAL A/C

So far we were dealing with sizing for continuous steady state power. Motor driven appliances (such as refrigerators and air conditioners) require larger amounts of current to start-up. This is because induction motors initially act like a short-circuited transformer. The maximum start up current is referred to as "Locked Rotor Amps" (LRA) because initially the rotor is at rest. This current will drop significantly when rotor accelerates to about 75% full speed. The LRA is typically 3 to 8 times continuous operating current (called full load amps, or FLA). That's why if you have a large motor-driven appliance such as a central air conditioner, you have to consider surge current capability of a generator. You can usually find LRA value of an appliance on its motor's nameplate label. If the starting current is not stated on the label, see our chart below for typical nominal starting requirements of single-phase 240V central air conditioners depending on their size. By the way, this chart may be confusing if you try to use units' conversion factors. Indeed, technically, 1 ton refrigeration is 4.7 hp or 3.5 kW. However, in case of air conditioners, electricity is used only to pump energy from a cold area to a hot area. With typical a/c efficiency, 1 kW of electric power can actually transfer 3 to 4 kW of cooling. That's how 1 ton air conditioner can have only 1 hp motor.

Once you found LRA, you can add this extra current to your sizing requirements and pick a generator that can handle this current. However, there is one lesser known detail here. Most guides will tell you to pick a generator with surge current matching nominal LRA of your motor. With such an advice you may wind up with twice larger device than you really need. The case is that nameplate LRA is normally given for full voltage starting. In reality, if you start an a/c from a generator, the motor's current surge causes voltage dip of the generator. When the voltage drops, the motor's current is reduced proportionally. Most residential appliances can start with 30% voltage sag. It means they may draw 30% less starting current than their nameplate LRA. Note that commercial applications normally allow only 15% voltage drop.

Generator manufacturers often specify their models' surge wattage capability, but unfortunately, they rarely state surge current capability. Therefore we may need to calculate the required starting wattage. As we explained above, the starting current can be $0.7 \times LRA$ at 30% voltage drop. If it is a 240V appliance, the required starting wattage is $(0.7 \times LRA) \times (0.7 \times 240) = 117.6 \times LRA$ (volt-amps). If you are considering a particular series of generators and can't find data on its surge capability, you may use the chart below for ball park estimates.

A/C Cooling Capacity	Nominal BTU/ hour	Motor size, hp	Running kVA at 240V	Full load amps	LRA at 240V	Starting kVA @30% voltage dip
1 ton	12,000	1	1.2	5	33	3.9
2 ton	24,000	2	2.4	10	67	7.9
3 ton	36,000	3	3.6	15	100	11.8
4 ton	48,000	4	4.8	20	117	13.8
5 ton	60,000	5	6.0	25	145	17.1

Standby generator rated power (kW)	7	10	13	14	16	17	18	20
Surge current capability at 240V 1-Phase (Amps @ 30% Voltage Dip)	46	63	95	102	117	125	133	145

SIZING PROCEDURE:

1. Determine LRA of your central a/c either from its nameplate label or from our chart. If you use nameplate label, multiply the stated LRA by 0.7 for starting at 30% voltage sag.
2. Turn on all devices and lights that you want to operate in an emergency and measure continuous electric currents on both lines L1 and L2 as described above.
3. Take the largest of I1 or I2 and add extra surge current as a difference between LRA and rated current. This will be your required surge current.
4. If you want to find required generator's surge watts, multiply the result found in step 3 by 240×0.7=168 (volt).

Example. Suppose you have a 5-ton a/c and you found that in steady state operation your house consumes 40A from one line (L1) and 30A (L2) from the other one. From our table we find that at nominal voltage a 5-ton a/c has LRA=145A and operational current 25A. At 70% voltage LRA would be 145×0.7=101.5 A. This is extra

76.5 A relative to the rated current of 25A. So, we are adding 76.5A to 40A (which is largest among I1 and I2). This yields 116.5A. From the generator chart we see that such a surge current can be provided by systems rated 16 kW or greater. If you pick 16kW device, you would have up to 10 kW available to run other devices in your home since at steady state operation, the 5-ton a/c will consume about 6 kW.

Since generator manufacturers often provide starting watts rather than starting amps, in our example your starting watts requirements would be 240×0.7×116.5=19,572 W.

If you have several motor driven loads, the calculation is a bit more complicated. You will need to find the load with the greatest difference between surge and running currents. Then add that difference to the total running current of all appliances. This will give you net surge current requirement of your backup system under the assumption that multiple devices rarely start up at exactly the same time. Alternatively, you may choose to set your standby system to manual mode. Then in an emergency you could first turn on the appliance with the largest starting current and then all other loads sequentially.

HARD STARTING

If you already have a generator and it has problem starting up your central air conditioner, it may require some form of assisted starting. In this case, you may install a so-called "hard start" kit. **Be sure to remove power from the air conditioner for at least 10 minutes before you touch anything and be sure to wear line-worker's rubber gloves.** There are various types of starting kits. One type is a two-wire device that has to be connected with "piggy-back terminals" parallel to the existing "run capacitor" (these terminals may be marked RUN). Such a device normally has a large capacitor in series with a component that acts as solid-state relay. This "relay" is basically a material with a positive thermal coefficient (PTC). It rapidly increases in resistance as it is heated when an electric current passes through it. As the result, the PTC component disconnects the start capacitor from the circuit soon after power is applied. It then remains hot from the "trickle current" that continues to flow through it as long as there is voltage. Note that when the power is disconnected from the motor, the solid state material begins to cool down, which takes one to two minutes. If AC is re-applied during the cooling off period, the hard start capacitor may be ineffective because it is still disconnected. An example of such a PTC kit is Supco p/n SPP6, which costs about $15. Another type of hard start kit uses a potential relay with voltage or current sensing to determine when to disconnect the capacitor. Such a kit can have either two or three wires. The 3-wire device has to be connected to Common, Start and Run terminals. Your best bet is to call the a/c manufacturer and ask for suggested type of hard starter for your model.

SIZING A PORTABLE GENERATOR

Sizing a portable generator involves three main things:
- ✓ Choosing appliances you want to operate during a blackout;
- ✓ Finding power consumption of selected appliances;
- ✓ Determining a distribution of the selected appliances between two 120V outputs of generator.

As we mentioned above, wattage charts and calculators scattered throughout the web do not necessarily provide accurate information. When I surveyed online sizing guides of major generator manufacturers and retailers, I found for example, that a refrigerator wattage suggested by various sources varies from 132 W to 800 watt! In my view, the best way of determining how big a portable generator you need is to actually assess power consumption of your specific appliances.

One way of doing this is by looking at nameplate labels of your devices. Usually such a label provides rated current rather than power. In this case, you multiply this current by 120 if this device is plugged into a regular wall outlet, or by 240 if it runs off 240V. For example, if a label states that rated current is 10A and the device connects to 120V, then the consumed power will be 10x120=1200 volt-amps. Note that technically speaking, watts and volt-amps are not always equal- their ratio is called power factor. However single-phase generators are normally rated for unity power factor, so we can disregard the difference.

If it's difficult to reach the label, you can actually measure the power consumption of your device. It's much simpler than one might think. All you need is a portable meter called Kill-A-Watt® which sells for about $20. You just unplug your appliance from the wall outlet, plug the Kill-A-Watt into this outlet, and finally plug your appliance into the meter's receptacle. The screen of the meter will show you volt-amps consumed by your device (as well as other characteristics, such as power and kWh).

THE TRICKY PART

Once you know the power consumption of the devices you want to backup, the tricky part begins. You can't just add up all the numbers as most guides suggest. This is a common mistake! First you need to figure out how to distribute your loads between two 120V outputs of your generator. Let me explain this with the following example. Suppose you have three appliances consuming 1,500 W each. One would think you need a 4,500 W generator. Wrong! As we explained above, most generators in North America (except for very small ones) provide two 120V lines. The generator's rated power is split between these two lines. Each of them can supply not more than half of the generator's power. In our example, you would have to run two loads (totaling 3,000 W) off one output and one load (1500 W) off the other output. This means, you would need a generator whose each 120V output can supply 3,000 W. In other words, you would need a 3,000×2=6,000 watt generator rather than 4,500 W.

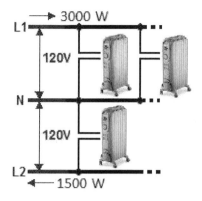

EXAMPLE.
IF YOU HAVE
THREE 1,500 WATT
APPLIANCES,
YOU NEED 6,000 W
GENERATOR (NOT
4,500 W).

Many guides suggest adding 10-20% to your power requirements for safety margin. It may be a good idea, but I personally don't think it is necessary, especially if you are on a tight budget. The thing is, compressors of refrigerators and air conditioners are continuously cycling on and off. It is highly unlikely that everything would operate at full load at the same time. Actually, the U.S. National Electrical Code (NEC®) 2014 recognizes this fact and in certain cases allows electrical system designers to use adjustment factors from 50 to 80% under assumption of load diversity of 50%.

AN IMPORTANT NOTE.

If you connect your portable generator via a transfer switch, you may not get your generator's full power. The case is, a portable generator connects to a transfer switch via its high-current 120/240V outlet. The problem is the ampacity of such outlets are usually lower than generator's ampacity. For example, a 10-kW generator can in theory provide up to $10,000W/240V=41.6$ amps. However, such a device typically has a 30-amp L14-30 outlet. This means, you can run only $240V\times30A=7,200$ watt through a transfer switch. To get the balance of the power (if you need it of course) you would still have to use extension cords. One of the largest (if not the largest) portable generator, Generac 5735 GP17500E rated for 17,500 watt, has a 50-amp NEMA 14-50R outlet. So, maximum you can get from it is $240V\times50A=12,000$ watt. Maybe that's why the inlets and most manual transfer switches do not exist above 50 A.

BATTERY-BASED BACKUP

There are three main disadvantages of all engine-driven generators:

- They emit toxic fumes and should be run only outdoors;
- They require frequent maintenance;
- They are very noisy.

Many portables generators (except for inverter-generators) have one more drawback: they produce low quality power, which may not be suitable for some sensitive electronics. That's why battery powered backup systems with inverters sound very appealing. Indeed, they have several advantages:

- Indoors operation;
- No pollution;
- Clean well-regulated power;
- No maintenance is required;
- Silent operation.

There are two basic types of residential battery powered backup systems.

PORTABLE BATTERY BACKUP.

Portable systems are powered from a wall outlet and provide electricity at their built-in AC receptacles. When utility voltage is present, they pass power through to connected equipment and at the same time keep their internal batteries charged. When electrical outage happens, an internal transfer relay switches the output receptacles to the inverter, which runs off the battery. Such systems are sometimes advertised as home battery backup. In reality, they are nothing else than uninterruptible power supplies (UPS) similar to those that are sold for computer applications. They do not provide power to the house wiring and backup only the devices that are plugged into them. In addition to this, the capacity of such corded systems is limited by the current one can draw from an AC outlet. Since a standard duplex wall outlet in North American homes NEMA 5-15R is rated at 15A maximum per each receptacle, you can't draw out of it more than $120 \times 15 = 1800$ volt-amp. A recommended continuous load is actually 80%, which is 1440 VA. An example of such a portable inverter with a transfer relay is Tripp Lite APS1250.

FIXED BATTERY-BASED SYSTEMS.

Such systems likewise contain a battery bank, a charger, and an inverter. However, unlike portable ones, they don't have a line cord and output receptacles. Instead, their AC output normally goes to terminal blocks, which have to be hardwired to the home electrical system. The AC input has to be hooked up after the main service disconnect. The AC output may be connected to an auxiliary electrical panel that contains critical electrical branches. When there is a grid failure, the internal transfer relay will automatically disconnect this sub-panel from the utility lines and connect it to the inverter. The inverter module usually includes the charger and the relay. An example of a hardwired inverter is Tripp Lite APS3636VR. The battery bank in such systems is usually external and may be sold separately. It can be scalable, so you can size it for a desired runtime.

Unfortunately, batteries used in the above applications have low energy density relative to other sources of energy. For illustration let's take for example Deka deep cycle battery 8G27. I picked this part number because its dimensions are similar to a typical car battery ($13 \times 7 \times 10$'). Its rated capacity is 72 amp-hours (AH) for 5-hour discharge. Of course, if you want to prolong a battery life you should not discharge it more than 50%, but let's ignore it for now. So, how do 72 AH translate to power? Since the battery nominal voltage is 12V, it will provide up to $72 \times 12 = 863$ watt-hours, which is $863/5 = 173$ watt for 5 hours. If your house consumes for example 5,000 watt you would need $5000/173 = 29$ such batteries for 5-hour backup. This is what a typical 5000 watt portable generator with a 7-gallon tank will normally provide per tankful. So, energy-wise 29 batteries are like 7 gallons of gasoline.

Let's consider another example. Tesla offers Powerwall system (44" x 29" x 5.5") with 13.5 kWh lithium-ion battery priced at about $6,600. Ignoring for a moment the losses in inverter and wiring, we can estimate that it would supply for example, 5000W roughly for just 13,500/5,000=2.7 hours. In contrast, a 5kW propane-powered generator can run about 10 hours from a single BBQ tank. Aside from high cost and low power density, consider the following. You can store some gasoline on site and re-fuel your generator, but to re-charge a battery you need electricity, which obviously will not be available during a blackout unless you carry it to some other area. That's why battery backup systems are not suitable for a long-term emergency. They may be good for short-term rolling blackouts with low power requirements, such as for emergency power for a computer workstation, modem, etc.

QUICK SELECTION CHECKLIST AND MY PICKS

I realize some folks don't have the time or desire to read long guides and would like to see just the conclusion. Some people may prefer that someone just tell them what to choose. This section provides quick recommendations on the selection of a generator for power outages as well as my picks. I will show what options are available-- you will still need to decide what level of protection you want and how much money you are willing to spend. Of course, what I say here is just my personal view- it does not constitute a professional advice.

CHEAP PORTABLE FOR A FEW CRITICAL APPLIANCES

For under $500 you can get a basic bare bone small portable device that provides 120V with up to 4,000 watt. It can run 2-3 "cord and plug" devices (such as a fridge and a room a/c). Just do yourself a favor and don't buy a gasoline-fuel model- after a major natural disaster gas may be difficult to obtain. A Consumer Reports survey of owners of portable models revealed that 22% of them ran out of fuel during 2012 storm Sandy. That's why my preferred choice of emergency fuel for a portable generator is propane. Dealers often keep filled BBQ tanks in stock and their refill does not require electricity. For this budget my pick is dual fuel Duromax XP4850EH (~$460), which comes with wheel kit and electric start. If it is not available, check out similar XP4400EH and XP5500EH.

PROS:
- Low cost;
- Can be used right out of the box.

CONS:
- With this size you may not get 120/240V (usually only 120V);

- You will need to move around a few hundred pound device and run extension cords through your windows or doors;
- It won't energize hard-wired appliances and lights unless you install an additional changeover system. And if you do install it, and your house has 120/240V service, you will feed only half of your lines.

MID-SIZE PORTABLE FOR SELECTED DEVICES AND LIGHTS

You can buy a 6 to 8 kW generator for under $1000. It will provide 120/240V and can power most home appliances, except for high-power ones (such as central a/c). In this category my pick is dual fuel Westinghouse WGen7500DF that sells for about $950. It provides 7500 watt on gasoline and 6750 watt on propane, includes wheels and remote start. My second choice is Champion 100165 with similar characteristics, but without remote start. You can use these gensets with extension cords just like smaller ones in the first option. However, for extra $500-$1,500 or so you can have a manual interlock or a transfer panel installed in your basement and pre-wired to selected lines and to an outdoor inlet. This arrangement will allow you to run most hardwired devices and lights.

PROS:
- With a transfer system you'll have to connect a single generator cable rather than many extension cords;
- You can energize fixed appliances and lights;
- Models in this range provide both 120V and 240V.

CONS:
- Higher cost;
- If you decide to install a transfer system it will obviously take a certain amount of time to get a required permit and to do the wiring.

Note. As I said above, I don't recommend gasoline-fired models. But what if you already have a gas generator and you worry that the fuel will not be available after a storm? If you are mechanically inclined and you don't mind forfeiting the manufacturing warranty, you can get a third party kit that converts a gasoline-powered engine to a multi-fuel one, which can run additionally on propane and natural gas. You may search web for the companies that sell such kits and check if they have one that will work with your particular model. I don't endorse these kits; but just wanted to mention this option.

AUTOMATIC STANDBY SYSTEM

If you prefer a convenience of fully automatic hands free operation with no refueling, and can spend overall from $6,000 to $13,000, you can go for a standby home generator system with an auto transfer switch. The generator is installed outside and will run from the fuel line you use for your home's heating, such as natural gas or propane. The transfer panel is mounted indoors. Residential grade stationary systems start at about $1,900 and may cost up to $6,000 depending on wattage, options, and manufacturer. You will also need to spend $4,000-$8,000 for electrical wiring and connection of the fuel line. The actual installation cost will depend on the project complexity, the length of the lines, and of course on the contractor you chose- get estimates from several installers. When you interview them, among other things, you may want to ask how many generators have they installed during the last year.

For the basic household needs I would choose 7.5kW Generac model 6898. It is one of the cheapest automatic home generators on the market, if not the cheapest one. It does not require high fuel rate and may likely run from your existing gas service. However, if you need to run a central a/c up to 5 ton you need a 15-17kW system. In this power range I would pick 16,000 watt Generac model 7036 or 20kW 7039. Again, before committing, be sure to check the capacity of your gas service meter- it should be imprinted on its nameplate. As I wrote above, most residential meters are rated 250 CFH or less. This is not enough for a large generator (see our chart for CFH requirements). Your gas utility may charge you anywhere from $100 to $5,000 to upgrade your meter- call them up to find out their fees.

PROS:

- Hands-free automatic operation;
- Practically unlimited runtime (except for oil change and maintenance interruptions);
- Lower noise.

CONS:

- Highest cost;
- It takes a certain amount of time to get a required permit and to do the installation of fuel line and transfer system.

ELECTRICAL REFERENCE

The main quantities of electric circuits are voltage, current and power. Ohm's law for resistive circuits states that the rate of the flow of electric current is equal to voltage divided by resistance: **I=V/R,** where I- current in amps, V- voltage in volts, R- resistance in ohms. Power is **P(watts) =VxI.**

Below is a so-called Ohm's law pie chart. It lets you calculate any quantity of electric circuit when you know any two other quantities. To use the chart, select in the center circle the quantity you want to find. Then select the formula containing the known values from the corresponding quadrant.

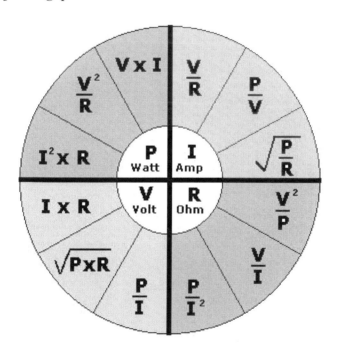

Example. An appliance draws 10A from 120 volt line. How much power does it consume? From the "11 o'clock" section of the chart we find: P=V×I, P=120x10=1200 watt. Technically speaking, the above relationships are valid for resistive loads. For circuits with so-called reactive elements (inductances and capacitances) we need to deal with impedances instead of resistances and with volt-amps instead of watts.

RELATIONSHIP BETWEEN SOME POWER AND ENERGY UNITS

Although casually the terms energy and power are used interchangeably, they are different quantities. Energy is the capacity for doing work. Power is the rate of doing work or the rate of using energy per unit time:

$$\textbf{Power}=\textbf{Energy/Time} \qquad \textbf{Energy}=\textbf{Power} \times \textbf{Time}$$

The **watt** (W) is the basic unit of power. By definition, 1 W equals to one joule (J) of energy per second. Joule is used primarily in science. Energy comes in many forms, such as heat, motion, gravitational, radiated solar power, and electrical. For different types of energy other physical units are also utilized. In electrical terms, one watt is produced or consumed when one ampere flows through a potential difference of one volt: **1 W = 1 V × 1 A**. Since for the electrical industry this unit is small, larger units are frequently used. For example, the kilowatt (kW) which is equal to one thousand watts is frequently used as a measure of residential electricity usage. The energy unit commonly used for electricity consumption is the kilowatt-hour (kWh), which is a measurement of a net electricity flow over given period of time: 1 kWh= Power(kW) × Times(hours). For example, a 100-W bulb in 10 hours will use 100×10=1000 watt-hour=1 kWh energy.

1 kilowatt (kW)= 1000 watt
1 British thermal unit (Btu)= 1055 J
1 watt= 3.41 Btu/hr
1 kilowatt-hour (kWh) = 3,412 Btu
1 horse-power (hp) = 746 watt
1 kilowatt = 1.34 hp.

LEGAL DISCLAIMER

All information in this book is provided "**AS IS**", reflects only the opinion of the author and do not constitute a professional or a legal advice. Do not use it without independent verification. The sole responsibility when buying or using a product rests with the buyer.

While the author used reasonable efforts to provide accurate information, he makes **no warranties or representations**, either express or implied, with respect to accuracy, applicability, fitness, or completeness of the information contained in this book. The author assumes **no liability** or responsibility for any error or omissions in the information contained in this book. In no event the author will be liable for any kind of damages, direct, indirect, punitive, incidental or consequential, arising out of the use of the information contained in this book.

Electric generators present carbon monoxide (CO) hazards. They also present the risk of fire, electric shock, or injury. Use them only for intended uses according to their operation manuals, NEC®, and local codes. The author specifically **disclaim any and all liabilities** associated with your dealing with any generator including those mentioned in this book.

If your state does not allow above exclusion of warranty or limitation of liability, then the above limitations or exclusions may not apply to you. In such a state the liability shall be limited to the greatest extent permitted by law.

ABOUT THE AUTHOR

Lazar Rozenblat is an electrical engineer with over 25 years of experience in the power electronics field. He lives in New York with his wife. He has two daughters and five grandchildren.